Original title:
Wealth of Self

Copyright © 2024 Creative Arts Management OÜ
All rights reserved.

Author: Tim Wood
ISBN HARDBACK: 978-9916-88-460-7
ISBN PAPERBACK: 978-9916-88-461-4

The Depths of Inner Peace

In silence lies the gentle breeze,
Where worries fade, and hearts find ease.
A tranquil mind, a soothing flow,
In depth we plunge, ourselves to know.

The stars above, they softly glow,
Guiding us where calm will grow.
In shadows deep, we learn to trust,
Our souls entwined, in peace we rust.

Embracing whispers of the night,
We find the spark, the inner light.
With every breath, we stand renewed,
In depths of peace, our fears subdued.

So close your eyes and drift away,
In stillness find the path to stay.
For in this space, all things align,
The depths of peace, pure and divine.

Seasons of Abundance

Spring blooms bright with colors bold,
Life awakens, stories told.
From winter's grasp, new growth appears,
In sunny days, we shed our fears.

Summer's warmth, a golden hue,
Nature gifts its vibrant view.
With laughter shared and joys amassed,
In moments rich, the die is cast.

As leaves turn gold in autumn's hand,
We gather fortunes from the land.
With hearts full, we give our thanks,
Embracing life, in shared ranks.

Winter brings a quiet grace,
In stillness, we find our place.
In every season, gifts unfold,
Abundance wrapped in love's pure gold.

Radiance from Within

In shadows deep, a spark ignites,
A glow that warms the coldest nights.
From hearts that beat with inner grace,
We find our truth, our rightful place.

With every breath, a light will shine,
As whispers call, our souls entwine.
Embrace the fire that lives inside,
For in our strength, we take great pride.

Echoes of Inner Prosperity

In the silence, wealth does grow,
Like rivers deep, its currents flow.
A garden sown with dreams and care,
The fruits of love beyond compare.

Each thought a seed in fertile ground,
Where echoes of our worth abound.
As gratitude weaves through the day,
We find abundance in our way.

The Gem of Self-Worth

Within the heart, a treasure lies,
A gem unseen by worldly eyes.
With every bruise, its luster grows,
In scars, the story of us shows.

We polish hope with gentle hands,
And nurture dreams where courage stands.
As we unveil our radiant core,
We celebrate what we adore.

Tapestry of Inner Light

Each thread a story, woven tight,
In hues of joy, in shades of light.
Together we create the scene,
A tapestry of what has been.

With every stitch, our souls align,
In patterns bold, our spirits shine.
Through woven paths, we find our way,
In unity, we greet the day.

Sparkling Shadows

In the dusk where whispers play,
The shadows dance and sway.
Stars above begin to gleam,
Painting softly our shared dream.

Moonbeams cast on leaves of green,
Silent tales of worlds unseen.
Candles flicker, spirits bright,
Guiding us through the tender night.

The Alchemy of Being

In the heart where gold unfolds,
Secrets of the soul retold.
Transmuting grief into pure light,
Weaving shadows into flight.

Each moment is a spark divine,
Transforming water into wine.
Within the chaos, find your song,
The alchemy of right and wrong.

Priceless Reflections

In mirrors deep, the truth does gleam,
Echoes of a lost, sweet dream.
Every flaw is a story told,
In the depths, our hearts behold.

Time's embrace, a gentle brush,
Turns the silence into hush.
In each wrinkle, wisdom lies,
Priceless tales beneath the skies.

The Abundance of Authenticity

In every voice, a rhythm flows,
Threads of truth that brightly glow.
Breaking masks and shedding fear,
The heart's pure song is what we hear.

When we stand in our own light,
Life becomes a vivid sight.
Embrace what makes your spirit free,
The abundance of authenticity.

Wealth Beneath the Surface

Beneath the waves, the colors gleam,
Hidden gems in a sunlit beam.
A treasure trove of stories told,
In the silence, rich and bold.

Among the rocks, the secrets hide,
Nature's riches, her gentle pride.
In every shell, a tale refined,
We find the wealth, the heart aligned.

The Dance of Authenticity

In every step, a truth unfolds,
A rhythm born, as life enfolds.
With every twirl, we shed the mask,
The essence clear, a simple task.

With open hearts, we join the flow,
Revealing selves we seldom show.
In every glance, in laughter's ring,
We find the joy that freedom brings.

Abundance Within

The garden blooms with seeds of grace,
Within the self, a sacred space.
In quiet moments, joy takes root,
A hidden wealth in every fruit.

In gratitude, the heart expands,
With open palms and gentle hands.
The flow of love, a boundless sea,
In mindfulness, we come to be.

The Treasure of Being

In every heartbeat, life's delight,
A gentle glow, a beacon bright.
In stillness, we uncover gold,
The treasure of the present holds.

With every breath, we weave the now,
A tapestry of sacred vows.
In moments simple, joy is found,
The treasure lies where love is crowned.

The Fount of Inner Peace

In silence deep, where shadows play,
I find my heart, I lose my way.
The stillness calls, a soft embrace,
Guiding me to my sacred space.

Beneath the stars, my worries fade,
In whispered dreams, the light cascades.
A gentle breeze, it stirs the night,
Awakening my spirit's flight.

A Symphony of Self-Discovery

Each note I play, a story told,
The melody of dreams unfold.
In every chord, I seek my sound,
A tapestry of me is found.

With every rise, and every fall,
I dance through life, I heed the call.
Exploring depths, I learn to see,
The vibrant song that sings in me.

The Opulence of Wisdom

Like rivers flow, through ages past,
The gems of thought, in shadows cast.
Each lesson learned, a treasure gained,
In quiet moments, wisdom reigned.

The quiet mind, a palace grand,
With every thought, a guiding hand.
The whispers soft, of time's embrace,
Reveal the truth in life's vast space.

Echoes of Abundance

In every breath, the world aligns,
With gratitude, my heart entwines.
The blessings flow, like rivers wide,
Abundance blooms, I feel the tide.

The sun will rise, the moon will glow,
In nature's arms, my spirit's flow.
Each moment rich, with gifts to share,
An echoing dance in cosmic care.

Collected Charms

In a jar upon the shelf,
Whispers of a hidden self.
Buttons, beads, and old twine,
Stories linger, tales divine.

Each charm a little spark,
Glimmers softly in the dark.
Treasures found in quiet lands,
Crafted with delicate hands.

Moments wrapped in faded thread,
Memories of what we said.
Through the years they softly gleam,
In shadowed corners, they dream.

Emblems of the Heart

Beneath the chest, a thumping drum,
Softly whispers, love will come.
Tattered letters filled with grace,
Embers glow in their embrace.

Each heartbeat, a gentle plea,
Words unspoken longing to be.
Tokens worn and deeply scarred,
Each moment cherished, each felt hard.

Fleeting glances weave the tale,
In silence, love, we set our sail.
Emblems of the heart entwined,
In every truth, a world defined.

The Mosaic of Me

Fragments bright, a myriad hue,
Sewn together, bold and true.
Pieces scattered, some in time,
Crafting life in rhythm and rhyme.

Shards of joy and shards of pain,
Each one tells a story's gain.
Colors dance in vibrant light,
Reflecting dreams both day and night.

In every crack, beauty shows,
Mosaic formed where the heart grows.
Unity in diversity,
The art of me, my tapestry.

Radiant Riches

Glistening gems of morning dew,
Nature's bounty, fresh and new.
Golden rays of sunlit beams,
Woven softly into dreams.

Fields of green, where shadows play,
Whispers of the earth on display.
Every leaf and every stone,
Riches that we can call our own.

Treasures lie in simple things,
The joy that every moment brings.
In hearts that shine with love so bright,
Radiant riches fill the night.

Celebrating Internal Prosperity

In the quiet of the mind, we grow,
Seeds of joy begin to sow.
Nurtured in our hearts, they bloom,
Filling life's canvas with their plume.

Gratitude lights the path we tread,
Each thought a whisper, gently said.
Embracing moments, small and grand,
We find true wealth, by choice we stand.

The wealth within, no gold can measure,
A treasure trove of simple pleasure.
With every breath, we celebrate,
The riches found in love's estate.

Sow the seeds and watch them rise,
Internal peace, the greatest prize.
In unity our spirits thrive,
A prosperous heart is truly alive.

The Essence of True Value

In shadows long where dreams reside,
True worth is found deep inside.
Not in things that shine and fade,
But in the love we freely trade.

The kindness shared on a quiet street,
The humble story at our feet.
Value lies in every touch,
In words of comfort, meaning much.

We measure life by moments spent,
In laughter shared, in time well lent.
In friendship's bond and family ties,
True value sparkles and never dies.

The essence glows, a gentle spark,
Illuminating even the dark.
In sincerity and in grace,
We find value in every face.

The Palette of Potential

Colors dance upon the page,
A canvas wide, a world to stage.
Each hue a whisper, every shade,
Dreams awaken, hopes unmade.

Brush strokes bold, or soft and light,
In potential's hands, we find our might.
The spectrum broad, yet focused thought,
In every moment, battles fought.

The red of passion, blue of calm,
Each color sings a soothing psalm.
With every blend, we craft our fate,
In this vibrant dance, we resonate.

From dark to light, our story flows,
Painting futures only we can impose.
In every choice, our spirit swells,
The palette of life, where potential dwells.

Aloud and Aware

In the silence, wisdom speaks,
Echoes of truth the heart seeks.
Awareness dances in the air,
A call to live, to feel, to care.

Voices merge in a gentle hum,
Together we rise, to overcome.
In every heartbeat, stories shared,
Aloud we breathe, together prepared.

With open eyes, we face the day,
Finding beauty in every sway.
In the stillness, life unfolds,
Awareness rich, a tale retold.

Let us be present, hold this space,
Embrace each moment, find our grace.
In harmony, our spirits claim,
Aloud and aware, we rise in flame.

Investment in the Soul

In quiet moments, seek the light,
Nurturing whispers in the night.
Each thought a seed, each breath a chance,
To grow amidst life's endless dance.

Wisdom gathered like morning dew,
A heart awakened, vibrant, true.
With patience sown, the soul will bloom,
A garden thriving, dispelling gloom.

In rows of kindness, love will thrive,
Each act of grace keeps dreams alive.
Invest in moments, small yet grand,
The wealth of spirit, hand in hand.

As time unfolds, the riches show,
In every heartbeat, beauty flows.
The soul's deep value, beyond the gold,
A treasure found, a story told.

The Bounty of Mindfulness

In stillness lies a precious gift,
The mind in flow, a gentle lift.
Awareness sharpens, senses wake,
A symphony in silence, hearts partake.

Each breath a brushstroke on the page,
Calm in chaos, wisdom's stage.
To savor moments, here and now,
In life's embrace, we learn the how.

With eyes wide open, beauty's near,
The mundane sparkles, crystal clear.
In mindful steps, with grace we tread,
A tapestry of life is spread.

Let thoughts drift softly like a stream,
In presence found, we weave the dream.
The bounty rich, in moments small,
Awakened souls, we share it all.

Crystals of Character

Each trait a facet, shining bright,
Reflecting values, pure and right.
In every action, choices made,
Like crystals formed, our truths displayed.

With strength of spirit, we endure,
Through trials faced, we learn what's pure.
Compassion's glow, a guiding star,
A beacon of hope, no matter how far.

Integrity, a sturdy stone,
In life's vast journey, we are not alone.
Building bridges with every deed,
Connecting hearts, fulfilling needs.

With patience carved, like ancient wood,
We grow in character, understood.
Each day a lesson, polished yet,
Crystals of character, we won't forget.

The Art of Self-Richness

In quiet places, treasures lie,
The richness found in the simplest sky.
With gratitude, our hearts expand,
Embracing life, a gentle hand.

To nurture dreams and set them free,
In every heartbeat, a symphony.
Creativity flows, a vibrant stream,
Painting existence, living the dream.

With time as currency, wisely spent,
Moments cherished, love's true intent.
In self-discovery, treasures unfold,
The art of richness, worth more than gold.

In kindness given, we're all enriched,
Connections deepened, souls stitched.
The canvas waits, so bold, so bright,
The art of self-richness, our guiding light.

Embracing Your Gold

In the heart, a glimmer shines,
Whispers of dreams in secret lines.
Each step forward, a dance so bold,
Embrace the value of your gold.

Golden moments, softly roam,
In your laughter, you find a home.
Trust the journey, let it unfold,
Together, we nurture what's gold.

Through storms that may come, stand tall,
Every struggle, a lesson we call.
With every scar, a story told,
Embrace the wealth of your gold.

In love and light, the truth we hold,
In every heartbeat, futures unfold.
Cherish the journey, let life behold,
A treasure found in embracing gold.

The Hidden Treasure Map

Buried beneath the sands of time,
Lies a map drawn in rhythm and rhyme.
With each marking, a tale to tell,
Adventure awaits, let your heart swell.

Paths less traveled, secrets await,
Just beyond the veil of fate.
Follow the signs with a heart so light,
Discover the treasures hidden from sight.

In shadows cast, the truth will gleam,
Trust in yourself, follow the dream.
Each corner turned, a choice in hand,
Unfolding wonders across the land.

As you venture through mist and wood,
Know that treasure comes when you've stood.
In every step, trust the intuitive tap,
You're the hero, the map's in your lap.

Echoes of Contentment

In the stillness, sweet whispers float,
Carried on winds, a soothing note.
Find joy in moments, small and slight,
Echoes of contentment, pure delight.

The sun dips low, painting the sky,
In hues of gold, as day waves goodbye.
Silent laughter fills the night,
In these echoes, life feels right.

Gather the stars, let them align,
In the quiet, your heart will shine.
With gratitude, let your spirit take flight,
Embracing the echoes, holding them tight.

Each breath a gift, each smile a sign,
In the tapestry of life, we intertwine.
Through love and peace, in the dim light,
We find our echoes in the starry night.

The Wealth in Authenticity

In a world where masks are worn,
Let your true self rise, reborn.
With open arms, embrace your light,
Authenticity, a glorious sight.

Let go of doubt, the chains that bind,
In your heart, the courage you'll find.
Each word you speak, let it be real,
In your truth, there's power to heal.

Celebrate quirks, the things that make,
A life well-lived, for your own sake.
In every moment, let your soul dance,
Wealth blooms within, give it a chance.

As you shine in your unique way,
You'll inspire others, come what may.
In the richness of honesty, feel the glee,
Authenticity sets the spirit free.

The Rich Tapestry of Life

Threads of joy and threads of pain,
Woven carefully, a sweet refrain.
Laughter dances, shadows play,
In this tapestry, night meets day.

Colors vibrant, rich and bold,
Stories shared, both new and old.
Every moment, a stitch we weave,
In the fabric of life, we believe.

Together we laugh, together we cry,
Underneath the vast, open sky.
Every heartbeat, a thread entwined,
In the tapestry, our souls aligned.

Through storms and sun, we find our way,
Crafting memories, come what may.
Life's a canvas, vast and wide,
In every heart, our dreams abide.

Embracing Inner Splendor

In the stillness, a whisper calls,
Echoes softly, within us all.
Layers peeling, revealing light,
Guiding paths through endless night.

Within the heart, a sacred flame,
A gentle spark, we can't contain.
Embrace the quiet, let it shine,
For in the depths, your truth aligns.

Dreams take flight, when fears release,
In self-discovery, we find peace.
Mirror of the soul, reflect your grace,
Embracing splendor, we find our place.

Look within, where treasures lie,
In every tear, a reason why.
Celebrate the magic, raw and real,
In this journey, we learn to heal.

The Odyssey Within

A voyage starts inside the mind,
Where cliffs of doubt and waves unwind.
With courage drawn from deep within,
Each step a dance, where dreams begin.

Charting paths through shadows vast,
Embracing moments, spellbinding, fast.
With every heartbeat, a story sings,
In the odyssey, we find our wings.

Lost in thought, yet never stray,
Building bridges, day by day.
Through storms and trials, truths unfold,
In the heart's compass, visions bold.

Search the depths, where secrets dwell,
In whispered tales, we weave our spell.
Journey far, but know it's true,
The greatest odyssey starts with you.

Everlasting Treasures

In every smile, a treasure gleams,
In shared silence, the heart redeems.
Moments captured, memories flow,
In the depths of love, we come to know.

Time may pass with fleeting grace,
Yet in our hearts, we find a place.
Friendship's glow, a guiding star,
In every tear, we've traveled far.

Hope's embrace, a gentle guide,
Through every storm, we walk with pride.
The treasure's worth is never measured,
In kindness given, life's true pleasure.

Collect the moments, hold them tight,
In every dawn, a brand new light.
Everlasting treasures, we can find,
In the love we share, forever entwined.

Treasures Within

In the quiet corners of the mind,
Awakens joy we often blind.
Whispers of dreams, softly unfold,
Hidden treasures, worth more than gold.

In shadows' dance and light's embrace,
Beauty lingers, a gentle trace.
Each thought a gem, each tear a pearl,
In stillness, we find our inner world.

With patience, the heart learns to see,
The wonders that shine, wild and free.
Within us lies a sacred song,
Where every note makes us strong.

So dig deep and uncover the light,
In the darkest hours, take flight.
For treasures thrive where waters run deep,
In the soul, great riches we keep.

The Gold in Solitude

In the stillness of the night,
Solitude blooms, pure and bright.
Thoughts like stars begin to rise,
Filling the silence, they harmonize.

Time slows down, each tick a gift,
In this space, spirits lift.
Amidst the quiet, wisdom grows,
In solitude, the heart knows.

Moments whisper, sweet and clear,
The secrets of life, drawing near.
For in the silence, we are whole,
Finding the truth deep in the soul.

Embrace the gold found in still air,
Where thoughts can weave their gentle care.
In solitude's embrace, feel the spark,
Illuminate the path, light the dark.

Mirror of Abundance

Reflecting dreams in crystal clear,
A mirror shows what we hold dear.
Abundance flows in waves of grace,
In every heart, a sacred space.

Looking closely, we can find,
The wealth of love that soothes the mind.
In gratitude, each moment gleams,
Filling our life with vibrant dreams.

For nature sings in colors bright,
A tapestry of pure delight.
The mirror speaks, of joys unseen,
In every soul, a vibrant sheen.

See the riches life imparts,
In the dance of open hearts.
Within this mirror, true wealth lies,
Reflecting hope beneath the skies.

Jewel of the Heart

Shining brightly, love's sweet grace,
A jewel dwells in each warm embrace.
Hidden deep, but always near,
The essence of hope, flickers clear.

Through every trial, bonds grow strong,
A treasure found where we belong.
In laughter shared and tears bestowed,
The heart's jewel lights the road.

With every beat, it sings a song,
Of unity where we belong.
In kindness wrapped, its warmth a balm,
A gentle touch, comforting and calm.

Cherish this jewel, bright and rare,
In every moment, love to share.
For in the heart, life's greatest art,
Is found within the jewel of the heart.

The Universe Within

In the quiet of the night,
Stars whisper tales of old,
Galaxies spin with delight,
Secrets of the heart unfold.

From atoms to vast skies,
We are made of cosmic dust,
Endless wonder in our eyes,
In this, we place our trust.

Every heartbeat a ripple,
In the fabric of the sphere,
Within us, worlds are simple,
Echoing the void so near.

As we soar through our dreams,
Branches of fate intertwine,
Life's a dance of endless themes,
In the universe, we shine.

Portrait of Purpose

Brush strokes of hope and grace,
On the canvas of our soul,
Every moment finds its place,
In the quest to be whole.

A journey painted with light,
Each decision, a bold hue,
In shadows, the truth ignites,
Guiding the heart anew.

With passion, the palette grows,
Dreams blend in vibrant flow,
In the contrast, purpose shows,
A masterpiece to bestow.

Through trials, the colors blend,
Each layer tells a tale,
Life's portrait, we defend,
With love, we shall prevail.

The Crown of Individuality

Every soul a unique crown,
Shaped by trials and by tears,
In the silence, we won't drown,
Our voice shines through the years.

Diverse paths we each have tread,
In unity we find our might,
Different stories, yet we spread,
A tapestry of pure light.

Embrace the quirks that you own,
Let your spirit dance and fly,
In the seeds of self, we've sown,
Individuality's high.

Together in our greatness,
Like stars in the night's embrace,
We rise up without sadness,
Each distinct, yet all in place.

The Abundant Mind

In the garden of thoughts, we sow,
Ideas bloom and intertwine,
From the seeds, we watch them grow,
A fertile land that's divine.

Imagination's endless stream,
Cultivating dreams with care,
Each vision a radiant beam,
Lighting pathways everywhere.

Creativity flows like a brook,
With every twist, it surprises,
In the pages of each book,
New horizons arise, no disguises.

With gratitude, our minds expand,
In abundance, we take flight,
In this vast, enchanted land,
Thoughts take wing into the night.

The Currency of Joy

Joy is a treasure, rare and bright,
It lights our days, a pure delight.
In laughter's echo, in love's embrace,
We find the wealth that time can't erase.

Moments we share, each one a gem,
Rich in memories, a precious stem.
In simple pleasures, our spirits soar,
The currency of joy, we can't ignore.

With every heartbeat, we trade our fears,
For fleeting moments, for laughter and cheers.
A smile exchanged, a hand held tight,
In the currency of joy, we find our light.

So gather these treasures, hold them near,
In this vast world, let love steer.
For in this dance, this joyful song,
We find our place, where we belong.

Glistening Spirit

In quiet whispers, the spirit gleams,
Shimmering softly, like sunlit streams.
With every heartbeat, it starts to glow,
A radiant force that we all know.

Through darkest nights, it finds a way,
Guiding our hearts to break of day.
In every challenge, it stands so tall,
A glistening spirit, lifting us all.

With dreams as our wings, we soar above,
Embracing the world, in light and love.
Each step we take, a journey bright,
With glistening spirits, we ignite the night.

So cherish this glow, let it expand,
Together we'll rise, hand in hand.
With every soul, a shining thread,
In life's grand tapestry, we are led.

The Luxury of Knowing

In depths of thought, there lies a grace,
A luxury found in a mindful space.
With open hearts, we seek the truth,
The wisdom gathered in the bloom of youth.

To question gently, to ponder deep,
In knowing's embrace, our secrets keep.
Each nugget cherished, each lesson learned,
In the luxury of knowing, our spirits turned.

Through time we grow, through challenges face,
In understanding's glow, we find our place.
For knowledge shared is a bond that's strong,
In the luxury of knowing, we all belong.

So let us wander through realms of thought,
In the tapestry of wisdom, we are caught.
With every insight, with every spark,
We illuminate the world, igniting the dark.

Embrace of Abundance

In fields of plenty, blessings grow,
An embrace of abundance, all can know.
With open arms, the heart receives,
In life's great bounty, the spirit believes.

Each gift that comes, we hold so dear,
In laughter and love, in joy and cheer.
With every sunrise, a chance to see,
The riches surrounding, wild and free.

So gather these moments, let them bloom,
In the embrace of abundance, life finds room.
With gratitude whispered, we rise each day,
In this vibrant dance, we find our way.

Embrace the waves, let them flow,
In the sea of plenty, let your heart grow.
For in sharing love, in giving, we find,
The embrace of abundance, forever kind.

Threads of Worth

In shadows deep, the threads we weave,
A tapestry of dreams we believe.
Each strand a story, vibrant and bright,
A testament to our inner light.

From doubts that cling, we start to rise,
With every stitch, we claim the skies.
Unraveling fears, we stitch anew,
A quilt of courage, strong and true.

In the loom of life, we find our place,
Embracing flaws, we learn with grace.
With every loop, we mend and bind,
Threads of worth, uniquely defined.

So let us thread our hearts with care,
And celebrate the love we share.
For in this fabric, rich and rare,
Lies the essence of who we dare.

The Spectrum of Self-Love

In the mirror, a rainbow glows,
Each hue a truth, as love bestows.
From crimson joy to azure peace,
In every shade, our hearts find release.

Emerald whispers of gentle thoughts,
Golden moments that life has caught.
Violet dreams that dance in the night,
Self-love blooms, a beautiful sight.

Through amber trials and sapphire tears,
We embrace each color, face our fears.
A spectrum wide, we learn to see,
The lavender light of being free.

So paint your world with love's sweet brush,
In every tone, let spirits hush.
For in this palette, vast and deep,
The spectrum of self-love, ours to keep.

The Heart's Arsenal

In the chambers where secrets dwell,
Lies the heart's arsenal, stories to tell.
With courage as armor and hope as a shield,
We face the battles, our fates revealed.

Each weapon forged from love's embrace,
With kindness and patience, we find our space.
Resilience grows in the heat of the fight,
As we stand together, igniting the light.

In moments of doubt, we summon the strength,
To navigate trials, go to great lengths.
Through arrows of grace, we pierce the night,
The heart's arsenal, ready and bright.

So heed the call, let courage arise,
Together we conquer, together we rise.
In the heart's vast arsenal, love leads the way,
A fortress of strength, come what may.

Navigating the Inner Landscape

In the quiet of mind, a landscape unfolds,
Mountains of dreams and valleys of old.
Through rivers of thought and forests of time,
We wander the paths, seeking the rhyme.

With each step taken, we find our ground,
In whispers of solace, peace can be found.
The horizon calls with a gentle embrace,
As we navigate this sacred space.

Through storms of worry and skies of gray,
We chart the course, come what may.
With compass of hope and map of the soul,
The inner landscape makes us whole.

So journey within, where treasures await,
Embrace the journey, don't hesitate.
For in this terrain, we learn to see,
The beauty of self, forever free.

The Currency of Confidence

In shadows cast by doubt's embrace,
We seek the light, a brighter place.
With every step, we rise and stand,
Confidence grows, a steady hand.

For whispers soft can turn to roars,
Breaking chains, unlocking doors.
Each challenge faced, a chance to soar,
The heart beats strong, we ask for more.

In moments claimed, we find our worth,
Like seeds of strength that sprout from earth.
The currency we hold inside,
In trusting self, we learn to ride.

With open hearts, we take the leap,
The dreams we chase, a promise deep.
For in our souls, a fire burns,
The currency of self returns.

Inner Gold

Deep within lies treasure bright,
A spark that glows, a guiding light.
Through valleys low and mountains high,
We seek the gold, we dare to try.

In silence found, in whispers heard,
We listen close, we take each word.
For every doubt that drapes the mind,
A gem of truth we're sure to find.

With each small step, we pave the way,
Unraveling fears that lead astray.
The golden whispers only grow,
Unlocking paths we long to know.

As layers peel, the light shines through,
Inner gold reveals the you.
A wealth of love that can't deceive,
In treasure found, we truly believe.

Harvesting Happiness

In fields of dreams where hopes align,
We plant the seeds of joy divine.
With care we water, nurture, tend,
Harvesting happiness, our true friend.

Through sunny days and storms that rage,
We cultivate, turn every page.
The fruits of laughter, sweet and rare,
In moments shared, love fills the air.

With open hearts, we gather near,
In simple joys, our souls draw cheer.
Each precious smile, a harvest gold,
In unity, our stories told.

As seasons change and years unfold,
We gather tales of love untold.
In every heart, a garden blooms,
Where happiness forever looms.

The Jewel of Self-Acceptance

In mirrors kissed by truths unmasked,
We find the love we've always asked.
With every flaw, a story told,
The jewel of self, a heart of gold.

In shadows past, we learn to see,
The beauty lies in you and me.
Through whispered doubts and silent fears,
We rise anew, in joy, not tears.

Embrace each part, the light, the dark,
In every scar, we find a spark.
For in acceptance, we reclaim,
The precious jewel of our own name.

Each day unfolds a chance to grow,
To love ourselves, the greatest flow.
With every breath, we stand so tall,
The jewel of self, the best of all.

Blossoming from Within

In the silence, seeds take flight,
Each petal whispers, soft and bright.
Dreams unfold in gentle rays,
Beauty blooms in quiet ways.

Hearts awaken, softly sing,
Nurtured by the hope of spring.
Roots entwined with earth's embrace,
Finding light in every space.

From shadows deep, the colors rise,
Painting joy across the skies.
In the garden of our mind,
Wisdom waits for us to find.

With every breath, we grow and change,
In the cycles, we rearrange.
Blossoming in perfect time,
Nature's rhythm, pure, sublime.

The Opulence of Intuition

Soft whispers dance upon the air,
Guiding hearts to places rare.
In the stillness, truths arise,
The soul's compass never lies.

Like rivers flowing, deep and wide,
Wisdom swells with every tide.
Trust the echoes of your heart,
In its language, we take part.

Shimmering light in shadows cast,
Illuminates the roads we've passed.
In silence, hear the sacred call,
The opulence is there for all.

Follow threads of ancient lore,
Unlock the secrets at your door.
Embrace the journey, one with you,
Intuition guides us true.

Roots of Resilience

In the storm, we bend but stay,
Roots run deep in life's ballet.
Through the struggle, rise and grow,
Strength emerges from the low.

Every scar a tale to tell,
In the cracks, we learn to swell.
Nurtured by the tears we shed,
Hope's the thread where dreams are led.

Branches stretch toward the sun,
Every challenge, we have won.
From the earth, we draw our power,
Blooming bold in every hour.

Through the fire, we ignite,
Resilience shines, a guiding light.
In unity, we find our ways,
Roots of strength for all our days.

Threads of Inner Harmony

In the tapestry of thought,
Woven dreams with lessons sought.
Each thread a moment, rich and wise,
Creating peace as chaos dies.

Colors blend in soft embrace,
Finding balance, finding grace.
With each heartbeat, gently steer,
Crafting harmony from fear.

In reflection, find the tone,
Join the notes, you're not alone.
A symphony within us swells,
In our hearts, the music dwells.

Threads of love weave all we know,
Binding us in radiant glow.
Together, we create the art,
Of inner harmony, one heart.

Unseen Affluence

In shadows where the riches gleam,
A heart of gold, a hidden dream.
Soft whispers of a life well-spent,
In laughter shared, where time is lent.

Beyond the grasp of worldly things,
The joy of love, the peace it brings.
Each smile a treasure, every tear
Adds weight to fortune held most dear.

Count not the coins or empty fame,
But cherish bonds that bear your name.
In silence find the wealth you seek,
A gentle pulse in moments meek.

So tread the paths of unseen grace,
In simple joys, you'll find your place.
For true affluence lies beneath,
In hearts entwined, in love's warm sheath.

The Priceless Journey

With every step along the way,
A lesson learned, come what may.
The road may twist, the skies may gray,
Yet hope will guide, a light to stay.

Through valleys deep and mountains high,
The spirit blooms, it learns to fly.
The struggles faced become the song,
In every note, where we belong.

Collecting moments, weaving dreams,
In laughter's echo, sunlight beams.
No map can chart the depths we roam,
For heart's true wealth will lead us home.

So cherish this, the winds that blow,
In every twist, the chance to grow.
Through trials steep, the canvas vast,
The priceless journey holds us fast.

Melody of Inner Wealth

In quiet whispers, soft and clear,
A melody that draws you near.
The notes of kindness, sweet and true,
Compose the song of me and you.

Resonate with love's embrace,
A harmony that finds its place.
In every heartbeat, find the tune,
A symphony beneath the moon.

Through laughter light and sorrows deep,
The music plays, the memories keep.
In every chord, a chance to grow,
The wealth within begins to show.

So let your spirit freely sway,
To joyful rhythms, come what may.
The melody of life shall rise,
A treasure found beyond the skies.

The Sanctuary of Self

In stillness lies a sacred space,
Where thoughts can wander, fears erase.
The whispers soft, a calming shore,
A sanctuary, forevermore.

Clothed in silence, wisdom waits,
Embracing peace, as love creates.
In solitude, the soul can thrive,
To nurture dreams, to feel alive.

With every breath, a chance to heal,
In tender moments, truth reveals.
The heart's retreat, where shadows fade,
In sacred stillness, joy is made.

So venture forth, to find your core,
In sanctuary, seek and explore.
For within you lies the key,
To unlock all that's meant to be.

The Legacy of Love

In whispers soft, the echoes play,
Each heartbeat shared, a bright array.
Found in the gaze, the warmth, the fire,
A timeless bond that never tires.

Through trials faced and storms defied,
With open hearts, we stand beside.
Each lesson learned, a gentle touch,
Love's legacy remains, our crutch.

In laughter shared and tears we sow,
A garden blooms, with love to grow.
The tales we tell, of lives entwined,
Unraveled threads, so rare to find.

A tapestry of moments dear,
In every stitch, the past is near.
As time unfolds, the story's spun,
Our legacy lives, we are but one.

The Bank of Dreams

In shadows deep, where wishes lie,
A hidden vault beneath the sky.
Each dream a coin, both bright and rare,
Invest in hope, breathe in the air.

With every thought, a value grows,
A treasure chest where courage flows.
The heart's desires, a grand estate,
In joy, we cultivate our fate.

The currency of love and trust,
In every moment, we are thrust.
A wealth of visions, bold and true,
The bank of dreams awaits for you.

So sow your seeds and watch them sprout,
In every doubt, cast fears out.
For in this haven, bright and bold,
Your dreams are worth their weight in gold.

Unveiling Inner Riches

Within the soul, a treasure shines,
In quiet depths, where wisdom binds.
Each thought a gem, each feeling rare,
A wealth that blooms, beyond compare.

As layers peel, the truths unfold,
Within our hearts, the world we hold.
In kindness sown, in love we find,
The riches born of the shared mind.

Unravel knots of fear and doubt,
In every whisper, hear the shout.
For inner strength can never fade,
A boundless light in shadows laid.

In seeking self, we find the grace,
To navigate life's fierce embrace.
Unveiling depths, we learn to see,
Our inner riches, wild and free.

Inheritance of Joy

From roots of laughter, seeds are sown,
In every smile, the joy is grown.
Through simple acts, joy finds its way,
An inheritance, day by day.

In moments shared, in stories told,
We pass it down, a warmth to hold.
The giggles echo, the hearts ignite,
A legacy of pure delight.

As sunshine breaks through clouds of gray,
We dance in light, come what may.
To cherish life and all it brings,
An inheritance wrapped in wings.

So let us sing, in harmony,
The gift of joy, forever free.
In every heartbeat, let it flow,
An inheritance of joy to grow.

Richness of Being

In the heart of life's embrace,
Moments weave a soft grace.
Colors dance in fleeting light,
Each day's gift, pure delight.

Whispers of the morning sun,
Raindrops fall, life has begun.
Every breath, a treasure found,
In stillness, joy knows no bound.

Gentle laughter fills the air,
Every smile, a silent prayer.
In the chaos, find your song,
Know, dear soul, you belong.

Embrace the present, hold it near,
Richness blooms when love is sheer.
In this world, both wide and deep,
Awake, alive, and free to leap.

Inner Equinox

In shadows deep, a light awaits,
Balance found as heart relates.
The quiet speaks in tones so clear,
In stillness born, we conquer fear.

Morning dawns with vibrant hue,
A dance of suns, a sky of blue.
Within the soul, two forces merge,
In harmony, we find our surge.

Stars above, they guide the way,
Night's calm whispers softly sway.
In every breath, the tides align,
The sacred space, forever mine.

Embrace the ebb, respect the flow,
In the center, let wisdom grow.
With each heartbeat, find your peace,
In the balance, find release.

Harvest of Dreams

Fields of gold beneath the sun,
Whispers of hope, journeys begun.
Each seed sown in fertile ground,
Promises in silence found.

Winds of change, they softly call,
As shadows grow and sunlight falls.
In the stillness, visions grow,
Nurtured souls in twilight glow.

Hands that toil, hearts that dare,
Gathering dreams from thin air.
In every heartbeat, magic swells,
Echoes of what the spirit tells.

As seasons turn, the heart expands,
A bounty held in loving hands.
In this dance of give and take,
We reap the joy that we awake.

Fortune in Silence

In the stillness, truth reveals,
Quiet moments, the spirit heals.
A gentle breath, a whispered thought,
In silence, all we seek is caught.

The world may roar, but here I stand,
Listening close, I understand.
Every sigh, a sacred space,
In stillness lies our highest grace.

Words unspoken, louder still,
In the calm, we find our will.
The echo of a knowing heart,
In every pause, a brand new start.

Fortune found when voices cease,
In quietude, we find our peace.
So linger long, let silence reign,
In stillness, joy will remain.

Gold in the Heart

Deep within where silence sleeps,
A treasure rare that softly weeps.
In laughter's glow, in sorrow's fray,
Gold in the heart will light the way.

Each gentle touch, each whispered prayer,
Turns shadows bright from dark despair.
The weight of love cannot be bought,
In every heart, true gold is wrought.

Through trials faced and dreams pursued,
In every moment, gratitude.
Though storms may come, they cannot part,
The endless gold found in the heart.

So let it shine, let it unfold,
This precious light, worth more than gold.
In each embrace, in every sigh,
The gold in hearts will never die.

The Richness of Spirit

In quiet moments, wisdom flows,
A tapestry of life, who knows?
With every breath, each thought we share,
The richness blooms beyond compare.

Through kindness shown and laughter's song,
In unity where we belong.
The spirit thrives in love's warm light,
A treasure chest that feels just right.

The heart that's open knows no bounds,
In every person, joy abounds.
With gratitude, we learn to see,
The wealth of spirit sets us free.

So let us dance in vibrant hues,
Embrace the rich, the old, the new.
In simple things, let beauty show,
The riches of spirit, always glow.

Soul's Bounty

Within the depths, our souls reside,
A bounty vast, a wondrous guide.
With every dream and hope we weave,
The soul's bounty we receive.

In laughter shared, in tears we find,
The treasures held, both rare and kind.
Each lesson learned, each moment dear,
In the soul's bounty, love draws near.

The courage found in darkest days,
The light that breaks through shadowed ways.
In every challenge, strength will sprout,
The bounty whispers, never doubt.

So with each step, let's sow the seeds,
Of kindness, love, and heartfelt deeds.
In every heart, there's space to grow,
The soul's bounty, let it flow.

Hidden Gems of Identity

In every glance, a story hides,
A labyrinth where truth abides.
Each facet shines in vibrant light,
Hidden gems of identity, bright.

Through cultures rich and voices true,
We find ourselves, a varied hue.
In shared experience, roots extend,
To celebrate, to love, to mend.

The past we carry, woven tight,
With threads of hope and shared delight.
In unity, we find our way,
Hidden gems, our hearts convey.

So let us seek in every face,
The beauty found in our own space.
Together strong, we shine and blend,
Hidden gems of identity, our friend.

Luminescence of the Mind

In shadows cast by doubt so deep,
A spark ignites, awake from sleep.
Thoughts dance like fireflies in the night,
Illuminating paths with gentle light.

Whispers of wisdom softly guide,
Through winding roads, an inner tide.
Each revelation, a color so bright,
Painting visions in the mind's soft sight.

Echoes linger, memories reside,
In the quiet corners where dreams glide.
A tapestry woven, thoughts align,
The brilliance shines—this mind of mine.

So wave your wand, let magic flow,
In every heartbeat, let courage grow.
For in the depth of the mind's embrace,
Lies endless wonder, an infinite space.

The Vault of Values

A treasure chest, where virtues hide,
In silent chambers, where hearts abide.
Honesty glimmers, a steadfast gold,
Love's gentle warmth, a story told.

Courage stands tall, a pillar strong,
Through tempest storms, it rights each wrong.
Compassion flows like rivers wide,
In the vault of values, we confide.

Integrity's light, a brilliant flame,
Guides us through life without shame.
Together they form a sacred trust,
In this vault of values, we must.

Honor those gems, let them shine bright,
For in their glow, we find our light.
Each principle nurtures the spirit's climb,
Creating harmony, transcending time.

Navigating Inner Riches

A compass points to the heart's own core,
Mapping treasures we all adore.
Hidden valleys and mountains high,
Where dreams awaken, and hopes can fly.

In silence, listen to the soul's soft call,
The wealth of wisdom, a bounty for all.
With every breath, it's plain to see,
Navigating riches that set us free.

Through forests dense where shadows play,
Find the gold in the light of day.
Each moment cherished, a jewel refined,
In the landscape vast of the seeking mind.

Let kindness be the map you draw,
And gratitude shape every flaw.
For in this journey, the heart will find,
The true abundance of the kindest mind.

Tapestry of the Heart

Threads of colors, woven tight,
In the fabric of love, pure and bright.
Each stitch a moment, a glance, a word,
In the quiet places where feelings stirred.

Laughter echoes in gentle lace,
Joyful patterns, soft embrace.
Through trials sewn with care and grace,
The tapestry grows in sacred space.

A splash of sorrow, a dash of cheer,
Each fiber tells stories that persevere.
Intertwined with hope, a vibrant art,
Crafting the story of the human heart.

Together we weave, in daylight's glow,
Creating a masterpiece as we grow.
In this tapestry, we find our part,
An eternal bond, the tapestry of the heart.

Radiance of the Soul

In the quiet depths, a light does gleam,
Whispers of hope, like a gentle dream.
Through shadows cast, the heart will glow,
Embracing warmth, in the ebb and flow.

Each thought a spark, igniting the vast,
Moments of peace, in the present cast.
With every breath, the spirit sings,
A symphony born on ethereal wings.

Awake from slumber, rise up anew,
Unveil the beauty, the world so true.
In the radiance, we find our way,
Guided by love, come what may.

Hold close the light, let it not fade,
For within the soul, true warmth is laid.
Together we shine, a beacon bright,
In the boundless night, we share our light.

The Fortune of Understanding

In the depths of thought, wisdom unfolds,
Tales of the past, in silence told.
Through the lens of love, we start to see,
The fortune of understanding, sets us free.

With open hearts, and minds so wide,
We navigate waters, with empathy as guide.
Every question asked, a treasure unraveled,
In the dance of discourse, our paths traveled.

Bridges we build, in kindness shared,
Together we rise, hearts fully bared.
In moments of solace, we find our way,
The fortune of understanding, here to stay.

Hand in hand, let us wander forth,
Inspiring hope, unearthing worth.
To seek and embrace, this beautiful art,
Of understanding each other, heart to heart.

Affluence in Simplicity

In quiet moments, life does reside,
A dance of joy, with nothing to hide.
Through simple pleasures, we find our song,
An abundance of love, where we belong.

The gentle breeze, the rustle of leaves,
In nature's embrace, the spirit believes.
A cup of tea, beneath the vast sky,
In simplicity's arms, our hearts learn to fly.

Each little moment, a gem to behold,
In the tapestry woven, with threads of gold.
From laughter shared, to the stillness we keep,
The wealth of our lives, in memories we reap.

So let us cherish, the small and the bright,
In the canvas of life, our colors ignite.
For affluence whispers, in every small thing,
In the heart of simplicity, our spirits take wing.

The Priceless Essence

In the depths of being, lies a treasure rare,
A whisper of truth, in the open air.
The priceless essence, in each heartbeat,
A dance of existence, so tender, so sweet.

Through trials faced, and joys embraced,
In the fabric of life, we find our place.
Like dew on petals, in morning's warm glow,
The essence of life, in each moment flows.

In laughter and tears, we discover the grace,
The beauty of journeys, each step we trace.
With love as our compass, guiding us near,
The priceless essence, always sincere.

So cherish the moments, both big and small,
In the tapestry woven, they matter to all.
For the essence of life, in kindness we share,
Transforms all our shadows, a light everywhere.

The Scarcity of Comparison

In a world of shining light,
We chase the shadows we create.
With every glance, a heart takes flight,
Yet binds itself to strange fate.

A mirror reflects what we can't see,
Judging worth on borrowed scales.
But beauty blooms in unity,
Not in the tales of others' trails.

To stand alone is brave and bold,
Let not comparison ensnare.
Within your story, life unfolds,
Unique, a treasure we all share.

So cherish the path that you have grown,
In authenticity, find your song.
For the true worth is never loaned,
In your own rhythm, you belong.

Cultivating Inner Gardens

In quiet corners of the soul,
Seeds of hope begin to sprout.
With care, we nourish our whole,
In tender whispers, we find out.

Each thought a flower, sweet and bright,
Dreams take root in sunlit space.
Through rain and shadow, find your light,
In every petal, find your grace.

We've all the tools, our hearts the spade,
To cultivate a life of bloom.
Let love be what remains unswayed,
In gardens rich, dispel the gloom.

So tend your spirit, let it grow,
Nurture warmth in every sigh.
For in the stillness, life will show,
A vibrant world that means to fly.

The Symphony of Self

In harmony, our voices soar,
Each note a truth that's ours to sing.
With every heart, a wondrous core,
Creating life from which we bring.

The bass of dreams, the treble's play,
In unison, we dance with fate.
Together in this grand ballet,
We craft a tune that resonates.

Within the silence, echoes ring,
The symphony, a shared embrace.
Listen close, for love will cling,
In every heart, a sacred space.

So play your part, embrace the score,
For every soul has a role to fill.
In this vast piece, forevermore,
Let joy resound, and time stand still.

Portraits of Wholeness

In colors bright, each stroke embodies,
The essence of who we aspire.
Every flaw and beauty, our bodies,
Create a canvas of true fire.

Each story etched, a life once lived,
In shades of sorrow and of cheer.
For every heartache, all we've given,
Forms the portrait we hold dear.

Unity lies in our disarray,
A tapestry of life we weave.
In each imperfection, find a way,
To celebrate what we believe.

So paint your truth with love's own hue,
Embrace the whole of who you are.
In the gallery of the living, too,
Stand proud, a bright, unyielding star.

The Gold Standard of Gratitude

In morning light, a spark of grace,
I count the joys that time won't erase.
Each smile bestowed, a treasure found,
In every heart, gratitude's sound.

The sun sets low, warmth in the air,
A gentle reminder to take some care.
For laughter shared, for love that binds,
In life's embrace, true wealth we find.

A whisper of thanks, a soft refrain,
In moments cherished, we lessen the pain.
With open hands, we gather the light,
In gratitude's glow, our spirits take flight.

So cultivate joy, let kindness grow,
In this gold standard, let love overflow.
For life's greatest gifts, we're never apart,
When gratitude glimmers within the heart.

The Lush Garden of Self

In quiet reflection, I tend to my soul,
Each thought a seed, each dream a goal.
With waters of kindness, I nourish my ground,
In the lush garden, true peace can be found.

The flowers of hope bloom in the dawn,
Each petal a story, a life reborn.
The weeds of doubt, I gently uproot,
As I walk this path, my spirit takes root.

Sunshine and rain, a dance on my skin,
With every storm, a chance to begin.
I cultivate strength, with thorns I've learned,
From the fires of struggle, my essence is burned.

In this sacred space, I flourish and thrive,
In the lush garden of self, I come alive.
With love as my compass, I'll always find peace,
As I blossom anew, my worries release.

The Wealth of Experience

Each moment a lesson, each tear a gem,
In the tapestry woven, I find my true stem.
Through laughter and sorrow, my heart learns to grow,
In the wealth of experience, wisdom will flow.

The paths that I've traveled, both rocky and clear,

Each whisper of time, a story to hear.
With every misstep, a dance with the past,
In the riches of memory, I find my steadfast.

The echoes of voices that guided my way,
In the shadows and light, they forever stay.
With gratitude flowing for each twist and turn,
In the wealth of experience, I brightly burn.

So cherish each lesson, both simple and grand,
For in every heartbeat, there's a master plan.
As I gather these treasures, I'll never grow old,
In the wealth of experience, my story unfolds.

Inner Sanctum of Strength

Within the silence, strength starts to rise,
In the inner sanctum, where courage defies.
Each challenge faced, a pillar anew,
In the heart of the storm, I find what is true.

Resilience blooms like a flower in night,
With roots that hold fast, and petals in flight.
The whispers of doubt are met with a smile,
In the sanctuary deep, I gather my style.

The echoes of struggle, I carry with pride,
For in every battle, my spirit's my guide.
With each rising dawn, I rise with the sun,
In the inner sanctum, my journey's begun.

So stand in your power, let the world see,
The strength that's within, wild and free.
For in the depths of the soul, the light is the spark,

In the inner sanctum of strength, I leave my mark.

The Currency of Kindness

A smile can light a shadowed face,
Small gestures weave a warm embrace.
In whispered words, true treasures dwell,
Each act of grace, a story to tell.

A helping hand in times of need,
Plants the seeds of love, indeed.
Riches not counted in coins or gold,
But in the kindness that we uphold.

Compassion shared, a gentle art,
Fosters connections that never part.
In every heart, a spark might grow,
When kindness flows, the world will glow.

Let's trade our worries for joy and care,
In the currency of kindness, we all share.
For in the end, what truly remains,
Is the love we give, in joyful refrains.

The Harvest of Self-Discovery

In quiet moments, truths arise,
Seeds of self beneath the skies.
Each strife endured, a lesson learned,
Through trials faced, our spirits burned.

A journey taken down winding paths,
In solitude, we confront our wrath.
The mirror shows both joy and pain,
In self-discovery, there's much to gain.

With open hearts, we collect our gains,
The echoes of laughter and remnants of pains.
Harvesting strengths from weakness' shroud,
Through introspection, we stand proud.

In the garden of life, we sow our dreams,
Revealing the truth in sunlight beams.
As we unearth who we are inside,
The harvest of self, our guiding tide.

Embers of Contentment

In gentle glow, the embers lie,
A warm embrace on a starlit sky.
In stillness found, we breathe the night,
Content in moments that feel just right.

The rush of life may pull away,
Yet peace prevails in simple play.
A cup of tea, a song we sing,
In little things, we find our spring.

Gratitude shines in the softest light,
Reminding us of joy, pure and bright.
With every breath, we choose to stay,
In the embers of contentment, come what may.

Let time unfold, we softly sway,
Trusted whispers will lead the way.
In heart's embrace, we find our home,
In embers low, we're never alone.

The Innate Fortune

In every soul, a treasure lies,
A spark of truth beneath the skies.
With gentle faith, we start to see,
The innate fortune dwelling free.

Through trials faced, and dreams pursued,
We learn that love is what is brewed.
In friendships forged and bonds that grow,
The greatest wealth is what we show.

For riches fade and time will wane,
But kindness thrives beyond the pain.
With every heartbeat, wealth we find,
In every stranger, a friend entwined.

So cherish moments, small yet grand,
For in the heart, true fortune stands.
With open arms, the world we greet,
In innate fortune, we feel complete.

Milton Keynes UK
Ingram Content Group UK Ltd.
UKHW032316121024
449481UK00011B/328